Zen Kitty

A Cat's Guide to Enlightenment

by Vanessa Sorensen

SOURCEBOOKS HYSTERIA™
AN IMPRINT OF SOURCEBOOKS, INC.®
NAPERVILLE, ILLINOIS

Published by Hysteria, an imprint of Sourcebooks, Inc.
P.O. Box 4410, Naperville, Illinois 60567-4410
(630) 961-3900
Fax: (630) 961-2168
www.sourcebooks.com

ISBN-13: 978-1-4022-0855-3
ISBN-10: 1-4022-0855-3

Printed and bound in China
LEO   10   9   8   7   6   5   4   3   2   1

To George, Sunshine, and Tom
For their love, inspiration, and generosity

What is the cat?
Elegance in form
Simplicity in movement

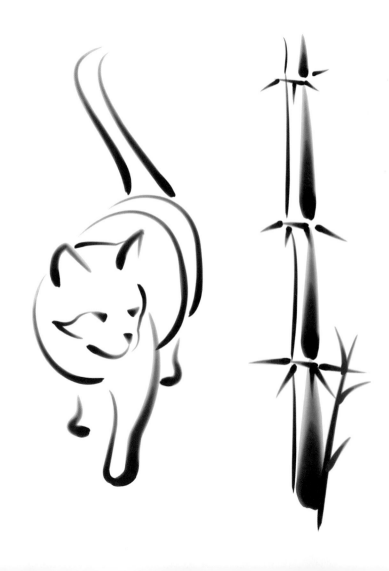

Remain flexible
To achieve
Your goal

Sit with dignity
Extend from center
Return to center

Every mark
On your canvas
Defines you

The key to happiness
Is learning
To let go

A gentle nudge
Is all it takes
To start a game

Soft pillow
Gentle kneading
Deep rumble from within

Dignity at all times
Is the true mark
Of a thoroughbred

Take time
And you will find
A world of wonders

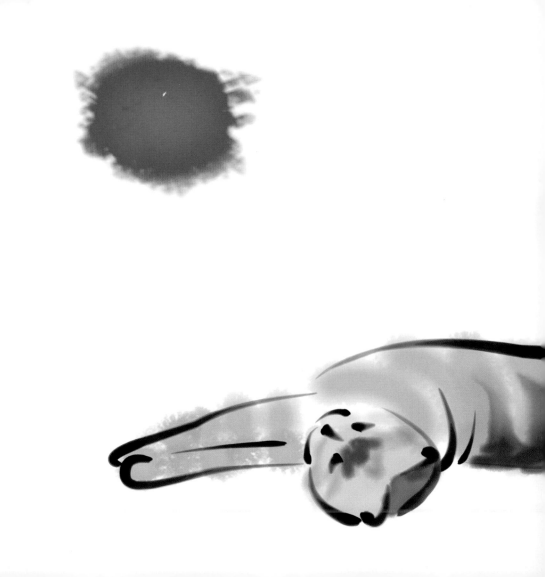

A good stretch
The sun on your fur
True contentment

A wise hunter
Knows his quarry
Like his best friend

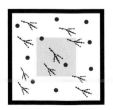

Overstimulated
I tear through the house
Safety under the bed

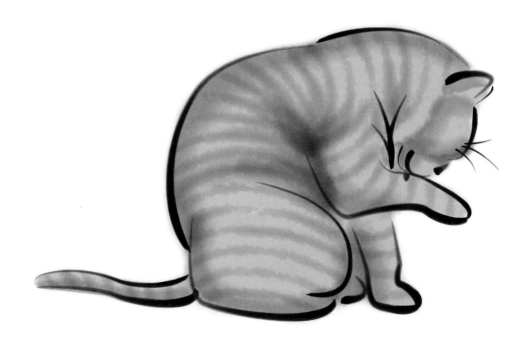

Your body
Is a temple
Treat it with care

Life
A swat of the claw
Death

To be thorough
I attempt to
Dig to China

Yesterday gone
Tomorrow unknown
Sleep now

A single flower
Can bring
Hours of pleasure

Listen to your body
For it will tell you
All you need to know

All things are possible
In the mind
Of the cat

To be safe
Think ahead
And behind

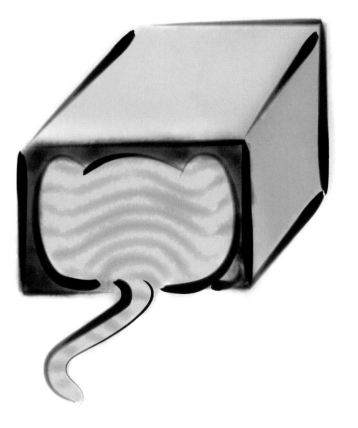

Big eyes
Small mouth
Good friend

Sleeping humans
Pounce
Awaken!

Be wary of those
Who follow
Too closely

In our imperfections
We may find
Unspeakable beauty

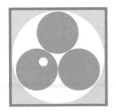

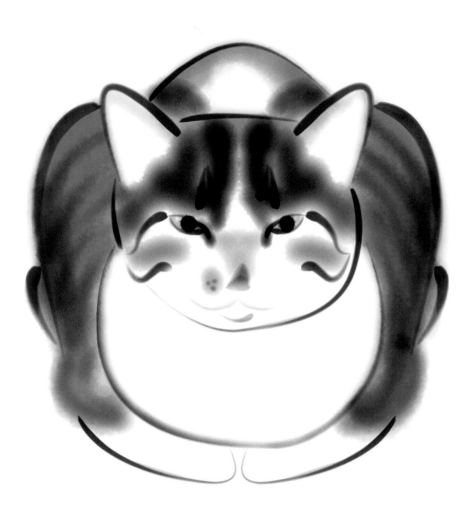

Only the fool
Overextends
To reach her goal

The wind blows
The last leaf falls
Winter approaches

Laser light
Someday
I will catch you

The wise
Look their enemy
Straight in the eye

Even the soft and furry
Must be approached
With caution

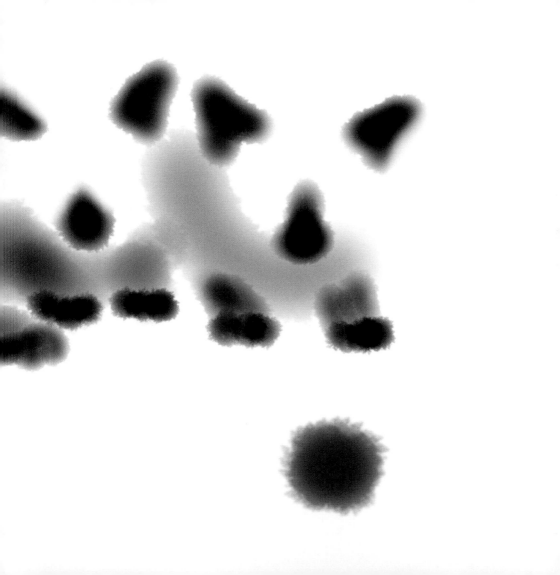

Everything has
A beginning
And an ending

About the Author

Vanessa Sorensen has a master's degree in zoology and works as a graphic designer. She lives in Cincinnati, Ohio.